The Baby Boomer's Guide to Life after Retirement

Changing the Way You Think About Life after Retirement

By: Julius Greene

9781681275246

Publishers Notes

Disclaimer – Speedy Publishing LLC

This publication is intended to provide helpful and informative material. It is not intended to diagnose, treat, cure, or prevent any health problem or condition, nor is intended to replace the advice of a physician. No action should be taken solely on the contents of this book. Always consult your physician or qualified health-care professional on any matters regarding your health and before adopting any suggestions in this book or drawing inferences from it.

The author and publisher specifically disclaim all responsibility for any liability, loss or risk, personal or otherwise, which is incurred as a consequence, directly or indirectly, from the use or application of any contents of this book.

Any and all product names referenced within this book are the trademarks of their respective owners. None of these owners have sponsored, authorized, endorsed, or approved this book.

Always read all information provided by the manufacturers' product labels before using their products. The author and publisher are not responsible for claims made by manufacturers.

This book was originally printed before 2014. This is an adapted reprint by Speedy Publishing LLC with newly updated content designed to help readers with much more accurate and timely information and data.

Speedy Publishing LLC

40 E Main Street, Newark, Delaware, 19711

Contact Us: 1-888-248-4521

Website: http://www.speedypublishing.co

REPRINTED Paperback Edition: 9781681275246:

Manufactured in the United States of America

Dedication

This book is in memory of my grandpa David. You are the coolest grandfather ever. Rock the heavens with your wits and awesome style.

TABLE OF CONTENTS

Chapter 1- Who are the Baby Boomers?... 5

Chapter 2- What Shaped a Baby Boomer's Life? 12

Chapter 3- Why it is Imperative to Act Today? 19

Chapter 4- Baby Boomers Beat Life Expectancy Rates.................. 25

Chapter 5- How Does a Baby Boomer's Brain Work? 29

Chapter 6 - The Proper Diet for Healthy Aging................................ 35

Chapter 7- Should You Supplement?... 41

Chapter 8- Exercise as Component to Health and Wellbeing 49

Chapter 9 - Your Financial Woes 59

Chapter 10 - A Lifestyle Makeover is Key to a Longer Life 64

Chapter 11 - Where Will Retirement Find You?............................... 70

Chapter 12 - Baby Boomer Grandparents.. 77

Chapter 13 - The 6 Baby Boomer Commandments......................... 83

About The Author.. 86

Chapter 1 - Who are the Baby Boomers?

The US registers the highest number of baby boomers, also called the Me Generation due to their tendency to focus on themselves and their needs, met in full by their parents who survived and prospered both economically and politically after the Second World War (1946). The children born to WW-II survivors were an enigmatic and interesting lot: with so much more freedom, financial security, social license and political changes happening around them, they took it much as their right to rule over making radical and revolutionary changes in the fabric of the society they lived in.

Thus, these youngsters were responsible for new-age thought processes, highly cultural leanings, being politically aware of civil rights and related issues that fuelled growth and development of the already affluent American nation.

Thanks to the increased birth rates registered between 1946 and 1960, America witnessed the highest number of baby boomers – the generation that challenged established norms, flouted conventions, sought answers and rode against the wave to empower their national economy and assist other global ones that were flagging, especially European ones.

Peace-time products and materials made in America were then shipped to other countries (ally nations) to support flagging economies, resulting in boosting business in the US and securing its citizens higher income jobs as well that enabled them to lead luxurious lives even after retirement. As a result, the standard of education and the lifestyle followed by the US families also registered a change for the better with baby boomers being able to afford more, earlier. Getting college degrees was easy and affordable for the highly paid families most baby boomers came from and so the US had more professionally qualified people joining its work-force and naturally became a super-power.

On the flip-side, with protests against Vietnam setting in, many of the young generation dodged drafting for military duty or did not show up after drafting, which was their way of recognizing communists and socialists as the bad guys and a means to become politically active was subsequently sought by them –through ensuring higher income jobs, which they excelled at. The baby boomer generation has political big-wigs like George W Bush and Bill Clinton among its dominant names, both of whom advocated and succeeded in leading America to the top with radical views and policies for boosting funds to the military services.

Julius Greene

Thus, with nearly 28% of the American population today comprising of baby boomers – the group defined as post WW-II babies who are now mature adults and retiring late, sustaining creative, business and personal energies for their further development, there is as much a boost to the government's decision making policies as much as there is concern over deciding changes for this generation's post-retirement health benefits planning.

Current changes on the anvil for the US government as far as baby boomers are concerned includes taking requisite steps for enhancing facilities for their healthcare budget and also for boosting their retirement benefits, 2 hitherto unexplored areas of progress for baby boomers and ensure national economic prosperity to be consistent.

The Australian Baby Boomer

There were 6 years in between 1945 and 1958 when due to conflicting political and economic issues, the baby boom had reduced considerably, but soon afterwards, childbirth rates in Australia continued to rise. Thus, essentially, the baby boomer years in Australia are officially tagged as being those between 1946 and 1961, which also witnessed a rise in the number of Europeans immigrants to the continent towards mid-20th century.

The '50's arrived with a bang for the baby boomers registered their presence everywhere in the business and educational world, having benefited from the booming economic prosperity of their parents who had survived the World War and additional advancements made towards medicine, science and technology fields.

The Baby Boomer's Guide to Life after Retirement

Among the major changes recorded in the social fabric of Australia during the time of the baby boomers were LP audio recordings in vinyl disc format,; '55 saw Bill Haley crooning 'Rock Around the Clock,' rock and roll became a national rage throughout the continent with local bands forming to dish it out to keen audiences and names like Johnny O'Keefe and Cole Joye emerging to be icons of the times. Blue jeans and tees became regular youth uniforms and American movie stars like Brando and Dean were hot favorites with the Australian baby boomer generation while the comic book craze of the US reached the land down under as well as other favorite American pastimes like Hula-hoops twirling, etc. which were different to the casual and conservative standards of the previous generation.

Along came the time for 'Beatle Mania' to official set in, in Australia; the '60's marked the UK pop boy-band touring Australia amid frantic fan followings turning into mobs crazed about their music as R 'N' R became 'in' and square parents who didn't quite fit the groove, were 'out.' Music brought in a new wave of change for Australian baby boomers with 'The Seekers' becoming the first local band to achieve the 1million mark in sales of records and Jeann Shrimpton raised more than a few eyebrows with her entry at the Melbourne Cup –dressed in a mini-skirt, which soon became all the rage. Social change set in by 1963 with aborigine activist, Charles Perkins, protesting and winning against racial discrimination in schools and social joints and enabling the entry of his people to established New South Wales's public areas and hitherto un-entered domains.

The '70s witnessed more socio-political changes post the Vietnam War and the protests against it: the Melbourne metropolitan was subsequently shut down following moratorium marches in opposition to it and brought in more power and awareness of self-growth for the baby boomers. Thus, with nearly 3million adult

Julius Greene

Australians during 1962-1972, the nation's conservative form of government had no choice but to give in the change first brought to life by Gough Whitlam, labor party leader and ideal Prime Ministerial candidate: some of his radical ideas included free education on a university, laws, an anti-discriminatory policy for Aborigines and calling back Australian soldiers from Vietnam. All of these were advocated and supported successfully by Australian new-age voters, who believed in freedom for all and utilizing creative energies for sustained development, in a peaceful environment.

The '80's saw these baby boomer radicals ageing but still in a position to enjoy the wealth and power accumulated over the years as even with their self-focus (the Me generation tag still sat heavy on the high income group), the Australian baby boomers continued to be prominent entities in the socio-economic and political fabric of the continent.

The Rise of the Independent Generation

The tern 'baby boomer' is the name given to the generation of people who were born right after the 2nd world war. That time of history saw over 70 million (70,000,000) Americans born to American citizens in the US. It really was a baby boom and the name stuck to anyone born during the baby boom years.

All those Americans born during the baby boom and are still living will now be in the age group of 42 to 60. This generation still plays a significant role in every political election in the country. And here in lies their power and importance, baby boomers plays a very important part in post-WW2 American history and has uplifted their generation to greater levels.

The Baby Boomer's Guide to Life after Retirement

Economic statistics are proof that all baby boomers in their 50's earn approximately 2 trillion U.S. Dollars. That accounts for over 77% of all the financial assets in America. As if that was not enough of achievement baby boomers have more than 50% discretionary authority in private organizations as well as in government.

What is of importance is that the baby boomer generation is now facing the issue of retirement since they are reaching superannuation. Financial constraints of retired life are the least of their worries, baby boomers are facing the emotional problem of dealing with the 'empty nest syndrome' – the feeling that takes over when their children grow up and go out to make a life of their own – on their own.

The empty nest syndrome sets in the same scenario when the baby boomer was newly married and setting out in life himself or herself. The difference is that this time round they have expended all energies and their youth is gone too. The baby boomer may deal with their emotions fairly well because they know they are looked up to and have to live up to their brand name – "The Independent Generation".

A poll that was conducted especially for baby boomers uncovered some very important points that are listed here:

1. The name of the baby boomer generation was drawn from the baby boom that followed the 2nd world war. All those born during the baby boom are called baby boomers.

2. Baby boomers currently account for 28 percent of the American population.

3. By 1957 it is believed that Americans gave birth to 4,300,000 (4.3 million) babies. It was in this year that the most babies were ever born in the United States.

4. Baby boomers look at superannuation with a positive vision rather than a depressed view. Many of the baby boomers plan to set up some profession or business even after retiring. Self-employment is the choice for a majority of baby boomers. Over 75% of the baby boomers want to also spend quality time with their families and mostly their grandchildren.

5. 50% of all the baby boomers are more than sure they will have adequate finances to enjoy a leisurely retired life, vacationing abroad is included.

Chapter 2- What Shaped a Baby Boomer's Life?

The 'Me Generation' or the Baby Boomers questioned existing political views, social stance and discriminatory laws in higher education besides channeling their creative energies towards boosting economic prosperity for the nation as they emerged successful in their chosen field through being over-achievers and leaders.

The year 1946 began with a bang for the baby boomers with some of the nation's biggest moments including Churchill's warnings about the 'iron curtain' of the Soviet controlling Eastern Europe; the UN's first general assembly, philanthropist, John D. Rockefeller donating his wealth to a New York-based UN headquarter and the Nuremburg war crimes being carried out, which resulted in 12 Nazis being sentenced to death.

Mahatma Gandhi, the charismatic Indian leader and advocate of peace and brotherhood was assassinated in 1948; communists in

Julius Greene

Czechoslovakian took over control of the land, the Marshall Plan was ratified, which approved of $17 billion being used for the aid of Europeans and Israel gave shelter to over 200,000 European refugees.

The following year witnessed the rise of communist power in China and its nationalists fleeing to Taiwan, the NATO being established and Israel becoming part of UN; Apartheid was officially declared as the governmental policy of South African, which was a feat for the global community that chose equality over racial discrimination.

The 1950's lot of baby boomers saw North Korea invading South Korea, Chinese communist forces taking over Tibet and President Truman and Alger Hiss being condemned on charges of perjury. The next year, the American Congress passed its 22nd Amendment allowing 2nd terms for a President while Ethel and Julius Rosenberg were convicted for passing on US nuclear to Soviet Union and President Dwight Eisenhower was elected to power the year after; the same year (1952) Princess Elizabeth was crowned queen of Great Britain and the U.S constructed Nautilus, its first nuclear submarine. 1953 came with its fair share of political upsets and victories, like Nikita Khrushchev winning after the death of Josef Stalin in the Soviet Union and Josef Tito being elected as the new Yugoslavian President; of course the execution of convicted spies, Ethel and Julius Rosenberg made headlines too while a laudable new branch, the U.S. Health and Human Services was also created.

1954 highlights included a Supreme Court verdict of racial discrimination in educational institutions being unconstitutional, Senator McCarthy conducting enquiries into the Army's communist infiltration and subsequently declaring it on national TV; '55 saw Martin Luther King, Jr., leading the 1st U.S. civil rights society and WW-II allies signing a treaty for restoring Austria's independence.

The Baby Boomer's Guide to Life after Retirement

The re-election of President Eisenhower made news in 1956 as did Israel's invasion of Sinai Peninsula, Fidel Castro starting off the Cuba revolution; ' was no less eventful: Eisenhower presented his 'Doctrine,' the Soviet Union brought in the space age via Sputnik and the last of the baby boomer years, 1958, recorded the US launching its first satellite, Explorer I while NASA was established and so was the United Arab Republic (with the coming together of Egypt, Sudan and U.S Marines intervention in Lebanon).

Thus, baby boomers sure grew up in interesting times.

The Typical Baby Boomer Injuries

When the US soldiers came back home after the Second World War, the period between 1946 and 1964 witnessed a population boom and the high birth rates marked the emergence of the 'Baby Boomer' generation, which contributed to the growing economic prosperity and change in political thinking in America.

Not only was financial wealth increasing with the baby boomers coming of age but due to the sustained support of their parents (the survivors of WW-II) in education, social life, public life and other aspects, this group was ready for all types of challenges thank to freedom of thought and action and the professional qualifications they were all armed with.

Independence and harnessing of creative energies was possible for the American baby boomers much in part due to their easy availability of college education and degrees, so now their generation (ranging between 42-60 years) is regarded as a keen subject for various studies, including the famous Windsor, Ontario one on how focused on their needs for improvement are – especially for fitness.

Julius Greene

A passion for exercising bordering on obsession may not be too out of line to describe the need of baby boomers to stay active and fit – and of course, an attempt to reverse the signs of ageing. There being such a things as 'too much of a good thing' not having occurred to many of the baby boomers lead to 'boomeritis,' a phrase coined to suggest the effect of existing too much on exercise.

The US Bureau of Labor Statistics studied efforts put in by health practitioners towards treating baby boomer injuries due to excessive stress on exercise and fitness and reports revealed an alarming 1million plus injuries recorded by their collectively putting in 488 million hours of labor for baby boomer patients in 2005 with an estimated $19,000 spent on their health management!

The Windsor, Ontario study reveals that baby boomers past the age of 50 are still pushing (or punishing) their bodies to exercise, which has resulted in giving rise to complaints of tendonitis, knee-problems and hip arthritis besides bursitis and other stressful health conditions; these combined fitness-related ailments has resulted in baby boomers over-doing the wear and tear their bodies can hardly put up with.

A rise in the number of hip and knee replacement surgeries between '95 and 2000 in the Windsor, Ontario Canada region points to this pathetic condition of fitness obsessed baby boomers suffering too many injuries, too frequently and thus, local health departments keen on educating this independent generation of go-getters advocate certain precautionary measures for aging baby boomers who'd like to stick to an active lifestyle – sans the disadvantages of injuries.

These tips for baby boomers keen to maintain fitness levels include choosing a form of exercise suited to individual health conditions, avoiding types of exercise that tire out their joints and learning to read body signals – meaning, easing off the regime when they experience pain.

In this manner, baby boomers high on the good effects of a regular exercise regime can hope to keep fit and healthy while also ensuring a balance between ways of producing healthy collagen levels (good for the cartilage) and eating a nutritious diet with plenty of Vitamin C and other healthy foods – but without compromising on the safety factor associated with sensible exercise. This requires proper warming up before entering into strenuous exercise routines, stretching for elasticity of muscles and using standard exercise gear and equipment for the work-out besides cooling down after the routine is over.

On Drug Abuse

Kids born after the Second World War were blessed with greater economic prosperity enjoyed by their parents who met their every need, from clothing to superior education, better lifestyle standards and thus, in turn, better chances at succeeding in the professional world. This generation made good use of the enhanced facilities offered them and the freedom made them question established norms, flout conventions and experiment with new-age thinking and products, including drugs and other mood enhancing substances.

Baby boomers were here to stay – and they made it known to the older generation how much they meant to be different and forward thinking by popularizing the use of marijuana and other prohibited substances. Their followers in turn, paid equal attention to drug-use and since this was a growing, indomitable breed of new-thinkers and radicals, in just a few decades, drug-abuse was rampant throughout American states.

Julius Greene

Experts like Joseph G forever reveal that survey material collected by The Substance Abuse and Mental Health Services Administration in the US have studied a similarity in patterns and trends of drug abuse in previous and current generations i.e. baby boomers and the generation after them. Statistics gained by these survey readings record baby boomers between 50 and 59 years of age revealing 4.4 per cent of them have used illicit drugs and teens in modern times (2005) have brought down this percentage by almost 10 percent. Perhaps, credit for this goes to awareness about drug abuse education spread by the government in public schools and social healthcare programs to discourage use of prohibitive drugs among the people besides efforts by the Office of National Drug Control Policy to highlight the ill-effects of smoking, alcohol abuse and use of illicit drugs like cocaine and marijuana.

The Asst. Gen. surgeon, Eric B. Broderick, questioned the shift in fundamental theories of youngsters (the 18-25 age-group) succumbing to peer pressure and subsequently adding on the amount of emotional baggage they bring with them to maturity, having experienced and experimented with illicit drugs. Murray, from the Office of National Drug Control Policy, names these as gauntlets and believes them to have doggedly pursued the baby boomers till the late 70s, which was undesirable for sustained growth.

Though many marijuana takers revealed they used illicit drugs by their own choice, others were supported in their quest for these substances through friends, dealers and relatives or even strangers sometimes.

According to John Walters of the National Drug Control Policy, baby boomers (nearly 78.2 million were born between 1946 and 1964) took drugs to such an extent that it became a part and parcel of their lifestyle, which was a hard habit to break. But, if Steve Hager,

The Baby Boomer's Guide to Life after Retirement

(Editor of High Times that advocates on marijuana), is to be believed, persons over 55 choose this substance over anti-depressants and sleep-inducing medication while those 5 years older still prefer to use drugs for pain and for treating glaucoma.

Smoking weed might have been the one thing when at Woodstock with many baby boomers admitting they are still hanging on to the habit till today, but Murray reveals a certain awareness about the ill-effects of drug abuse in the youth of today who do not want to make the mistakes their parents did and thus, are consciously avoiding the path of self-destruction that use of prohibited drugs can push them towards. Thus, the US government's health policies for future generations are sure to succeed with sensibilities changing and youth becoming more responsible towards their own future.

CHAPTER 3- WHY IT IS IMPERATIVE TO ACT TODAY?

Time is fleeting. It just doesn't last as long as we would like it to last. Although it may seem like just yesterday you were raising your children, those years have passed and now they are raising their own children. But, before you let any more time slip pass, start thinking of your future.

Although you may not be able to go back and adjust time, implementing the changes in your diet, your exercise, your mental health and in your financial health will allow you to find the necessary tools to excelling in your later years. If one thing is for sure it is that you can make a difference in the quality of the rest of your days if you take charge now, without wasting any more time.

What Kept You Busy Before?

Although you may be kicking yourself for not saving enough money or for not dropping those extra 40 pounds when you were younger, hold fast in the thought that you can still make progress by making changes today. In many ways, you'll be able to find the health and wellness that you could have had.

If you are younger, there are many changes that you can make today that will greatly impact your life later. In fact, if you simply make a few of these changes today, you'll be able to far exceed your goals in earning a savings account that can pay for retirement, in fending off heart disease and even keeping Alzheimer's at bay.

Every day that you implement positive change, is one more day that you have the ability to gain benefits. The sooner you start the more benefit you can obtain.

Why Change?

One of the largest in importance and probably the most difficult things to change is your mind.

Why can't I just live life the way that I want to today?

Why can't I just eat the foods that taste good and live the life that I am living?

What's going to happen if I do this for one more day, month or year?

You may not realize it, but each of these things can and will lead you to a premature death. Living one more day eating foods that are unhealthy will lead to the increased risk of heart disease. Living one more day with not getting enough sleep, not relieving stress and not getting the exercise you need, leads to disease and an immune system that can't keep up with you.

Julius Greene

Living one more day, takes off more time at the end. Is that really what you want?

There is good news, though. Most of the damage that you've done to your body can be reverse if you have done so in time and are dedicated to making that happen. With just a few minutes of care to your lifestyle each day, you can get back the time you may have possibly lost. Don't think that it has to be forever, because if you can change your mind, you can get it back.

Things to Change

You don't have to live a life that's super "clean" and yes, you can make mistakes, eat that fatty hamburger and still watch realty television if it makes you happy. But, the goal that should be realized is that these things should be done in moderation.

There are many things that you should take into consideration as being things to change. Here are a few of the most important considerations that you may have to make changes in.

1. Your Diet: Giving your body the nutrients it needs is vitally important to living as long as possible. Not only do you need to put good things in, but you need to get the bad things out. Giving your body the tools it needs to make this happen is important to living longer.

2. Your Brain. Stimulation to the brain needs to be on going. With the population's number of Alzheimer's cases expected to drastically increase with the Baby Boomer generation, it is virtually important that you provide the tools necessary to curb this if possible.

3. Your Finances. It is expected that in the next five years, more than 50 percent of those that enter retirement will not be able to support themselves but will rely on family, Social Security as well as charity. Is your financial future set for retirement?

4. Your Physical Fitness. It is critical that your body be physically fit. That means that the 2/3rds of the population in the United States that is overweight or obese needs to take heed. Heading into your later years with this type of physical problem will definitely shorten your life span.

5. Your Lifestyle. Getting social interaction, being happy, and less stressed are all key ingredients to a healthy and happy lifestyle. If you don't incorporate these types of interactions into your life, you lose mental alertness and your quality of life is just not what is should be.

Each of these five things can be changed in simple ways and in large ways to help you to prepare for the later years of your life. In fact, no matter where you are in your life, developing your own future is something you have the ability to change. That doesn't last forever, though.

Giving yourself an opportunity to excel is something you must do and you need to begin making the changes now. The good news is that we've broken it all down for you into a simple guide that will transform your life for the future.

What Societal Changes to Expect?

We look at this privileged generation that had its parents fulfilling their every need, right from giving them a sound education, higher college degrees, professional training, enabling them to focus on themselves and the freedom to make their own decisions that made the baby boomers an independent, entrepreneurial lot, filled with leadership skills, raring to go!

The baby boomer generation was very aware of the situation around them – be it political dead-locks, military drafting issues that they were not keen on, civil rights issues such as discrimination in education institutions on the basis of race and ethnicity – and they fought to bring in changes for a more equal, more American world. They also contributed in a big way to the industrial, academic and economic conditions of American and the US history is filled with tales of young, brave and free-thinking baby boomers that changed its course with their forward thinking, free-wheeling and highly unconventional ways to bring in and keep making money, all between 1946 and 1964!

The baby boomers grew up in times when civil rights were a big issue that affected everybody with their eyes open: protests, demonstrations, marches were in the face and soon they realized that more than the American Military regime it was the communists and socialists that were their enemies, so they grew more interested in learning to form their own political views and unafraid of airing them to educate the public about the ill-effects of the Cold War and impending Vietnam War issues.

Bill Clinton and President George W. Bush are 2 famous baby boomers with their distinct militarily and political views and even as one is a democrat and the other a republican, their views on empowering the military for retaining the US's status as a world power and matters of civil rights are pretty similar.

Coming to what the baby boomers want: in terms of this go-out-there-and-do-it-all generation, it would definitely mean better healthcare and medical aid facilities, now that many of them are facing retirement and post-retirement planning needs to be considered. Since life expectancy for the baby boomer generation has considerably increased thanks to advancements in science and medicine, it does mean that they need to be better prepared for living healthy, long lives and perhaps still contribute to the community around them with their creative energies – as many of them are keen to do.

With social security and medical healthcare taken care of, there's no reason why the baby boomers retiring today and cannot achieve all the retirement and health benefits they so deserve and travel, relax, rejuvenate and contribute to their community.

CHAPTER 4- BABY BOOMERS BEAT LIFE EXPECTANCY RATES

Walk into any department store and you'll find hundreds of beauty products lining the shelves. Each one of those products has something else, something unique to offer. Most promise to hide the signs of aging. Some make claims of being able to erase the years and to have you looking 10, 20 or more years younger. But, in truth, there is no way to avoid aging, is there?

Consider some numbers for a moment.

In the late 1800's and early 1900's, the average life expectancy in the United States was that of just 42 years of age! Today, that number has nearly doubled its size and that's no short feet to accomplish. The fact is that people are living longer because of the benefits of modern medicine and the benefits that technology offer.

In fact, today, there are over 70,000 people in the United States alone that are at the age of 100 or more! That is an outstanding number.

As you watch your parents' age, you are probably thinking to yourself the things that you would have done different, so that you don't walk down their same path.

Perhaps you would like to be more active so that arthritis doesn't set in so soon. Or, perhaps you would be tested sooner than they were for cancers, heart disease and countless other conditions. The good news is that you do have the ability to see these things going wrong and therefore you should be able to reach out and lengthen your lifespan.

One way we like to think that we can do this is by looking younger. That's why all of those products are on the market. If it was a multi-billion dollar business, there wouldn't be so many products trying to take part of that chunk of change. But, what type of anti-aging product can you possibly invest in that's going to improve the quality of your life?

What if we told you that it really had nothing to do with those products on the market, but that it had to do with the things that you are capable of making changes with today, right now?

With modern medicine and modern science, we have a much better understanding of how the things around use affect us. We know that cancer can be caused by toxins entering into your body when you breathe and we know that some forms of heart disease happen because of the foods we eat. But, we also know how virtually everything else on planet earth affects us too.

Chapter 5 - How Does a Baby Boomer's Brain Work?

Your brain is one of the most important things for you to take into consideration in any health regimen. For the Baby Boomer, it is even more vitally important to care for your brain.

Today, the number of Alzheimer's patients is quickly on the rise. There are numerous situations in which people are forced to realize that the years are slipping by and they no longer can keep a grasp on time.

There is no doubt that over time your brain is going decrease in function. You are going to lose some of its function over time. But, when that happens is what you should be worrying about.

With the right tools and planning, you can delay significantly these reductions. In some cases, you can even minimize the extent to which they happen to you. The good news is that the things that you can do to keep the mind stimulated and functioning correctly are things that are easy to do and even can be enjoyable.

There are a number of things you can do, actually, each of them offering their own benefit. Here are some.

Learning

Learning is one of the very best things you can do to your brain. As you age, many stop doing new things and looking for new areas of the world to explore. That is what starts the shutdown of the brain. Because you aren't using it as much, especially for new things, you aren't making it function as much as it needs to.

When you keep your brain functioning, you encourage it to continue to be active. On the other hand, if you don't, you lose the necessary functions that you need.

Some ideas here include taking a new class, learning to do something that you enjoy such as a new hobby, and even learning history. You can take courses at your local community college or start a discussion group about the books that you are reading. Learn to plan a new instrument. Learn to cook like a professional.

Stay Socially Active

Another thing that you need to do to help keep your brain healthy is to stay in the social scene. Involving yourself with others and keeping yourself part of the group helps your brain to function well beyond what it normally would.

If you become someone that lives alone, talks to no one and simply does the same things day in and day out, there is little hope that your brain will stay stimulated. But, encouraging your brain through relationship building, stimulation from others and just being with other people can help to keep your own brain active.

In addition, most people love to be around others and that in it can be a blessing to the brain. Doing things that you love improves your overall well-being.

Stay Physically Active

We've talked a lot about the need for physical activity but it is also important for your brain as well as the rest of your body. Because physical exercise stimulates circulation in your body, you'll actually be adding the circulation of blood to the brain. What's more is that if your body is physically active, your mind will be more likely to be physically active as well.

Doing the exercise regimens that are included here will help the Baby Boomer in body as well as in mind.

Brain Food

The nutrients that are required for your health and well-being are also important for your brain. It is essential that your body gets the right amount of nutrients for brain stimulation and health. One of the most important elements in that are Omega 3 fatty acids. These can be found heavily in fish or you can take them in supplemental form.

These nutrients are essential for the health of your brain. When you are developing the right supplement for your Baby Boomer body, it should include supplements for your Baby Boomer brain, too.

Keeping your brain active is very important to your overall well-being. Without taking in these considerations, you put your brain at risk for becoming ill and functioning less optimally. As you can see, though, this is one of the most prosperous and easy parts of the Baby Boomer's lifestyle that can be changed for the better!

How Do You Cope with Middle Age Dilemma?

It is a well-known fact that children love to celebrate their birthdays and these are occasions for calling in friends, having party games, special food and snacks besides other highlights such as clowns, party animal-rides and of course, decorations, cakes and gifts! However, as one naturally ages birthday celebrations get toned down and even people's attitudes towards growing older does; thus, even turning a year older can give some of the baby boomers a bit of a chill – aging is not something particularly loved by this 'Me Generation' and approaching 40, the thought of middle age can be very off-putting for them.

For some happy go lucky creatures, the idea of life beginning at 40 may keep them going strong but for others, the fear of aging is very deliberating, so they need to get advice and tips from those who have been there, done it – so they, too, can lead meaningful, fulfilling and whole lives.

Middle age comes with its own changes and demands, just like youth did: from emotional to mental to financial and medical, there's a gamut of aspects that need the baby boomer's attention and for the best of them to deal with these issues, requires proper knowledge and will power besides focus. Two important issues that often build up to a mid-life crisis are morality and aging: which are natural human aspects but can cause a major upset in the baby boomer, an individual accustomed to being treated highly, being independent and self-focused. The realization that these issues can also affect their families is another thought that eats into them.

Mid-life is generally tagged as the period between 40 to 60 and many baby boomers who have so far only focused on themselves, their goals and needs, now come to the realization of looking at factors they have directly or indirectly influenced, such as family, friends, colleagues and neighbors besides the community at large; so, they begin to take a more serious, introspective look at themselves and how they can bring fruitful changes to better these things around them.

Baby boomers grew up obsessed with exercise and fitness, endorsing and not afraid to use medical science's advances for getting that collagen treatment to reverse aging or keeping to a tight workout regime like jogging to keep the tires off; but sooner or later, they have to wake up and smell the coffee: which brings with it physical reminders staring the baby boomers right in the face. The mirror tells its true story for the baby boomers so afraid of aging and loss of hair, youthful skin, wrinkles etc. can be scary aspects of heralding another birthday.

They need to accept aging as a natural part of life and understand that all the anti-aging products of the biggest brands cannot stop birthdays from piling up or eventually showing up on the baby boomers' faces and bodies: emotionally, it can be more of a trying time for marriage partners, both of whom have aging issues and even end up in divorce if emotions are not kept in check. Being loving, encouraging about the changes and allowing a person to grow naturally into what they are meant to be is the understanding needed to keep relationships going: acceptance is the key element to aging and taking it gracefully and baby boomers in relationships need to be aware of this.

Of course, middle age is likely to bring along some unpalatable truths about your mortality: you'll come face to face with the reality of sagging skins, sun-spots, bags under the eyes, graying or thinning hair, even balding – weight gain and family drying around you will be difficult to deal with all together, but with determinations, foresight and a will to change your life around, you can be as productive as before and face mid-life: head-on!!

CHAPTER 6 - THE PROPER DIET FOR HEALTHY AGING

Here's an exercise for you.

What did you eat this morning or today, for that matter? Did you eat a well-balanced diet that's full of whole grains, lean proteins, vegetables and fruits?

Or, was your breakfast a cup of coffee and maybe a bagel, loaded with cream cheese of course?

You are what you eat. The Standard American Diet is a term that's been coined to describe the fast food crazy, greasy, fatty and high sugared diet that most Americans eat. Even if you live on the other side of the planet, chances are good that you aren't eating a diet that's rich in the foods that are important to your aging process.

In fact, the foods that you are eating that fall into that type of diet are what are playing the largest single part in killing you prematurely. As a Baby Boomer, you have plenty of life still left in you and your diet is the perfect place to begin making some serious changes. Just look at what it is doing to you!

If you have a larger midsection to your body, then you have a high risk of having a heart attack due to heart disease. Just a few extra pounds are all it takes.

If you consume a diet that is rich in salt, you are destroying your kidneys as well as some of the other organs in your body.

If you are eating fatty foods, you're killing you heart by suffocating it under layers of cholesterol.

What Diet Should I Follow?

If all of this scares you, which it should, you may be considering a diet. Yes, a diet does sound like a good idea but the problem with them is that it is ultimately impossible to stay on that diet for your lifetime. That leads to the potential for you not to follow it for long, allowing virtually none of the important benefits to come through to you. That's not what you want.

Diets that go from one extreme to the next are everywhere you look. Those that facing a diet that is high in protein are still putting their heart's at risk because of the increase cholesterol there. Those that are following a low fat diet are doing the opposite. They are not giving the body enough protein to build muscle mass, which actually helps you to burn fat faster.

Because diets are so extreme, they rarely work for people that are facing these conditions.

But, you don't have to face these problems to be able to gain the benefits that you need. In fact, the most basic of diets is one of the best ones to follow for your health and well-being.

Enter The Baby Boomer's Perfect Diet

Now, instead of thinking of this as a diet, think of it as a better way to eat. It is not something you'll ever come off of and it is not something that you should throw to the side. It is a way of life and although there are some things you will have to give up, it is still one of the easiest diets to follow.

In fact, if you do decide to eat something that you shouldn't, if you just go back to eating well from there out, you'll still be okay. It is all about controlling how much of the bad stuff you take in and making sure that the good stuff is what comes in more often than anything else.

Here's what you should be doing. Split up the foods that you eat into a pie graph. 50 percent of what you eat should be good carbohydrates. The next 25 percent of the foods you eat should be lean proteins. The final 25 percent should go to fats.

This way of eating is enjoyable and it's easy to follow. Here are some more specific points that you should install into your eating plan.

1. The carbohydrates that you consume should be made up of mostly fruits and vegetables.

2. The proteins that you eat should be from beans, tofu and other types of plant sources. About 1/3 of the protein you eat should come from animal meat and then it must be lean.

3. For fats, you want to obtain this from good fats such as olive oils and nuts instead of fats that come from animals. Look for poly and mono saturated fats for this section.

That's it. You pick the foods and as long as they fit within this diet regimen, you know you are working on creating a healthy and anti-aging diet that will propel you to health and wellness.

When to Eat Matters

It should be mentioned that you shouldn't sit down to a large meal, either. Instead, you should be eating four, five or even six smaller meals per day. One of the most important things that you need to "get over" when it comes to the food part of your life is that food doesn't have to be the center of attention. You need to disconnect the feeling of needing food to make you feel comfortable and relaxed. Learning this will be a requirement because you need to detach from the mentality of sitting down to a large meal.

If you have problems going from eating four to six small meals per day, try to add a fruit into your middle periods. This can help to stabilize your blood sugars to help you to feel better.

Getting Sugar Out

One of the key methods to improving your life for the future is to look at sugars. Refined sugar should be avoided at all costs. Why is sugar so bad for you? When you consume sugars, you are increasing the body's production of a substance that is called cortisol. That is a hormone that actually speeds up the aging process and can lead you to aging faster.

Now, to remove junk food from your body, you should start with the sweets. You don't want to excessively eat foods like junk food.

You also want to cut out the soda that you drink as that too can add refined sugar to your diet that you simply shouldn't have.

If you are craving something that is sweet, look towards healthy, whole fruits. Low sugar is better, but no sugar foods are even better for you.

Your Ideal Baby Boomer Weight

One thing that is a major difference from most other diets and weight loss plans is that with the Baby Boomer's Diet, you need to install a diet that allows you to drop weight. You should be looking to weigh about five to ten percent less than what you have been told your ideal weight is. That's not to say that you should starve yourself, but dropping these extra pounds will encourage a great deal of benefit in your body.

Here's a method to figuring this out that can help be a guide for you.

Women: The weight that you want to follow should be 100 pounds for your first five feet of height. Then, add on five pounds for every inch taller that you are.

Men: The weight that you want to follow should be 106 pounds for the first five feet that you are high and then an additional six pounds for every inch after that point of height.

Are you worried that you can't follow this type of diet? Do you think that it may be too restrictive of you? Remember that although this lifestyle is something that you should follow, that doesn't mean that it should be strictly followed without one falter.

The Baby Boomer's Guide to Life after Retirement

If it's your birthday, sure you want a piece of cake. Having a small piece of cake won't hurt you if you go back to your healthy Baby Boomer diet afterwards. If you have a sweet tooth, satisfy that sweet tooth with a piece of fruit instead of candy.

This coupled with a healthy diet will deliver for you the optimal health and wellness for years to come.

It is essential for you to make these diet changes so that your body doesn't take in the wrong things. You will see that if you adjust your diet to this type of plan that you will begin to feel good quickly.

Chapter 7 - Should You Supplement?

As a combination of the diet and exercise regimens of the Baby Boomer, it is also important to take into consideration supplementation and your body's hormones, both of which are critical at preserving the body's health and longevity.

You may ask why you need to add supplements to your diet when you have just started on a healthy diet that's been described here. The reason for this is really unfortunate for most.

Even with a healthy diet that is filled with just the nutrients from healthy food, you are still not getting all of the nutrients that you need to maintain optimal health. This is due to several key things including the way that your food is grown. For example, the way that your food is farmed has allowed for the soil to be depleted for many of the nutrients that you need. Many of these nutrients can actually help you to improve the longevity of your life.

Supplementation is needed for other reasons as well. Here are some examples of why you need to add the right nutrients to your diet now.

- Pesticides and herbicides are commonly used to help keep bugs off of the foods that are grown. While you think that this is a good thing, it still causes problems for the production of nutrients in the soil.

- The soil itself is often not even authentic soil! Some of the most modern farms are using synthetic types of soil which allow for faster and longer growing seasons that produce more products that's also good looking.

- With genetic mutation, scientists of have developed fruits and vegetables (not to mention virtually any other type of food that you eat) products that are genetically altered enough to produce the perfect specimen every time. The nutrients get left out.

As you can see, there are many reasons that the foods you eat don't have the nutrients that are needed to increase the longevity and health of your life. Still, you should also realize that even when you do get the right foods, you still have so many other factors that play a role in the way your body uses them. The sugars that you eat, the fats, and the high amounts of sodium cause the real nutrients to get lost in the mix. Your body doesn't get a chance to bring them in.

When you don't get the right types and amounts of nutrients, your body will break down faster with the onset of degenerative diseases. In fact, some studies have shown that with the proper nutrients you can die early. As you know, we are working on keeping you healthy, longer and supplementation can take us there.

What Do You Need In Supplements?

As we mentioned, it is quite important to insure that you are eating a healthy diet, like the Baby Boomer diet that we've described. But, in addition to that, supplementing your diet with the right vitamins and minerals will also be important.

Here are some things to remember about supplements in regards to what you should be consuming.

Select supplements that are right for your body. This should take into consideration your age, sex and your current health situation. Remember, you need to insure that the supplements you take will help improve the rate at which you are aging.

Antioxidants are an important part of the supplement that you take. Find one that offers a high amount of antioxidants which help to remove free radicals from your body. They help to deter diseases like heart disease and cancer. In addition, they help each of your organs to work better. Antioxidants also help to stimulate natural growth hormones to be released throughout your body.

You also want the supplement that you select to provide you with the necessary nutrients to help keep your organs running at the highest level. You want a product that will keep problems like heart disease at bay as well as Alzheimer's disease.

Mood benefiting products are also important. You want a product that will help to relieve stress and improving your general state of well-being.

The supplement that you take should also promote a healthy sex drive in both men and women. Not only is that something that you will want to have working optimally, but it also helps to secrete hormones that are necessary for health in the long term.

Look for a supplement that provides cellular rejuvenation. This means that the product will help in the restructure and repair of the cells of your body. You want the supplement to be able to promote this well-being in each of the cells of your body.

Your hair nails and skin should also be aided by the supplement hat you take. You want a product that will promote healthy skin cells and healthy, young looking nails and skin.

You should also look for the supplement to be a time released product as these generally are able to enter the body slowly and therefore are absorbed better into the body. Other products that are water soluble simply get washed away.

Finally, take the time to find out what's in the supplement. You want to find a supplement that is as natural in composition as possible. You should check to see if it has the Food and Drug Administration's seal of approval, but that is not always available.

Take the time you need to compare the products that are on the market. Instead of trying to find many supplements, each offering its own unique benefit, look for a supplement that features many of those that you need. A good place to start is to take your list of needs to your local nutritionist or to the health food store (you can shop for them online, too, of course!) Have them help you to find the perfect supplement for your anti-aging, health promotion.

Finally, when you get to the point of saying, "why am I doing this, again?" Consider this.

In the standard American diet, it would be necessary for you to consume a 5000 calorie diet in order to get the nutrients that you need for optimum health and even then some of them would be left out! Since the recommended diet is that of just 2000 calories (on the high side) you can see how this would be counterproductive to your efforts. Supplementation then, is a must.

A combination of healthy products is what you need to look for. That means vitamins and minerals but also herbal products. You'll find that the more natural the product is, the more benefits it can provide to your overall health and well-being.

Hormone Soup

The hormones that your body releases are very important to your well-being. As a Baby Boomer, you are likely already facing the depletion of the most important hormone in your body: growth hormone.

Growth hormone is important for a number of reasons. For one, it helps your body to grow and develop. But, it also helps to rejuvenate and repair the damage to your cells. In many ways, this growth hormone is responsible for the decline in your body over the years. It is, in short, what makes you look aged.

Now, if you could increase the amount of growth hormone in your body, you could potentially slow the aging process. In fact, those people that have the ability to live a life that has been riddled with all of the "bad stuff" and still somehow live to be 100 are telltale signs of this.

You see, in most people, the growth hormone that is so important to our longevity begins to taper off at the age of just 25! Each decade of your life, it will decrease yet another ten to fifteen percent leaving you with next to nothing. But, those that do live to see 100 are often a part of a small group of people that have a gene that keeps the growth hormone working optimally in their body for long after the point where most turn off, so to speak.

But, just because you don't have the ability to alter your genes doesn't mean that you can't help to keep growth hormone production happening in your body. No, we don't mean through artificial supplementation or any type of injections. You can do this through natural and non-side effect riddled ways.

If you did try to use an artificial type of supplementation of growth hormone, you would have to visit your doctor to get it. In addition, the wrong about can actually cause very severe side effects, including the possibility of death. Therefore, this is not the best way to get the growth hormone that is necessary for longevity.

You can, on the other hand, encourage your own glands to continue producing it. By stimulating the pituitary gland, you can actually allow it to begin providing your body with the necessary release of this hormone again. The type of product that you would use to make this happen is called secretagogues. These are all natural products which mean that they are generally safe to use, with few to no side effects.

Taking these supplements will help to provide you with some amazing benefits. You'll see improvements in your skin and in your hair first. You may even begin to have a sex drive again. By increasing your body's excretions of other hormones such as DHEA, progesterone and testosterone, it can also help improve the health and well-being of many aspects of your life.

Since your body requires hormones to help make things happen in your body, getting them to be balanced and secreted as they can be a wonderful thing for the rest of your body. For example, just increasing the right hormones in women after menopause can delay or even avoid osteoporosis, heart disease and even help to fend off cancers and other health concerns that you may have.

As you can see, with the help of secretagogues, you can find the benefits of health and well-being that you are seeking. To find these products, you can talk to your local health store or you can look for them available on the web.

Whatever you do, don't forget to include them in your diet and exercise regimen.

As you can see, the need for supplementation and for hormone stimulation is vitally important when it comes to maintaining your health for a longer period of time.

Although you may often be told that the things you do are what drive your age and how long you'll be healthy. But, there are factors that you can't control such as the growth hormone and the foods that you eat not having enough of the nutrients your body needs.

But, you can also see how you can repair these elements by simply including supplements into your diet. You'll also find that it is easy to tackle these problems once you have the right products to take.

The Baby Boomer's Guide to Life after Retirement

Yes, supplements may seem like a nuisance when you have to take them daily. But, adding a pill a day, so to speak, can really help to keep your organs working correction, keep your skin from looking aged and it can give you the nutrients you need to live a long and happy life. You definitely want that!

Chapter 8 - Exercise as Component to Health and Wellbeing

Everyone hates the word exercise, but it is a vitally important component to health and well-being. With so many people striving for improved health, there are gyms opening up everywhere. On top of this, you'll find countless opportunities to do simple exercise at home.

But, when we are talking about the health and wellness of the Baby Boomer, there is much more to it than just this. In fact, it is essential that you install a plan of overall exercise that incorporates several key types of exercise and movement.

Why Does Exercise Have To Matter?

Since we were children, we were encouraged to get outside and play. Today, the children that aren't doing this are unhealthy and overweight. Many have problems with learning and attention deficit problems. Much of this can be blamed on the fact that they don't get out there and play.

The Baby Boomer's Guide to Life after Retirement

As a Baby Boomer, it's important for you to realize that exercise can do many things for your health and well-being.

In fact exercise, when done correctly, will actually help you to look and feel younger.

Yes, this could be considered the anti-aging tool of a century because it can be that powerful when done correctly.

Have you ever been the type of person that did exercise regularly? If you ever went through a phase of going to the gym and working out, then you know that exercising does make you feel good. It makes you healthier too.

- You are stronger and therefore can accomplish more for longer periods of time.

- Your muscles are lean and fit, which means that they are less prone to injury or pain.

- Your body is working at optimal levels which help to keep the immune system working well.

- Your heart is working hard and therefore becoming stronger with each workout that you do.

- You are likely the right weight which means that you have less chance of heart attacks.

There are many ways that exercising makes a difference in the body and the Baby Boomer cannot ignore these facts if he or she is going to improve their overall health and well-being.

Julius Greene

Now, what do you need to do to gain the benefits that exercise can offer to you?

There are actually three key parts of the exercise regimen that you want to install into your life as part of your regular program. This is not a program that should be done only for a certain time period but over the course of your lifetime as long as your doctor approves of it.

By incorporating these key elements into your lifestyle, you will actually be building a healthier body that will live a longer and healthier life.

The three things that you must take into consideration include these:

- Your Heart: You need cardiovascular training that is centered on improving your heart's function.

- Your Muscles: Strength training is necessary for you. You need to improve the function of your muscles.

- Your Joints: Flexibility training increases the range of motion and discourages the onset of conditions such as arthritis.

If you don't believe that it's important to take into consideration any of these elements, consider these very frightening facts:

When you turn 60, you can look forward to having lost at least half of the strength you used to have. You also won't be able to count on not breaking a bone if you fall because your bones are much weaker. In addition, your lungs can't pump out nearly the amount of air as they used to.

But, if take the time to install an exercise regimen like the one we are encouraging you can completely wipe away these risks and improve your health and well-being considerably.

How to Do It

First and foremost you should see your doctor before starting any type of exercise regimen. This will insure that your body is healthy enough to handle what you are going to do to it. Don't worry; you won't be hurting yourself unless you don't take this first step.

Once you get the all clear from your doctor, you can begin at looking for solutions to your exercise needs. First, start by working on your heart.

Improving Heart Function

To do this, you'll want to take into consideration the aerobic exercises. If you get in an aerobic exercise program, you will help improve your heart considerably. During these workouts, you are pushing your heart to its limits. As you do that, you are also encouraging it to strengthen. Aerobic exercise improves your heart's function.

How much aerobics do you need to get in? For most people, it is necessary to do an aerobic exercise at least three times a week for at least 20 minutes per day. That's only one hour of your time that you are dedicating to aerobic exercise and you will see improvement.

But, for that improvement to happen, you do need to pay attention to what you are doing. In order to see benefits, you need to get your heart pumping at the right speed. To measure this, you will want to increase your exercise intensity to a level that is no more than 65 percent of your maximum heart rate.

To determine what that is, do this. Start with 220 and take away your age. Then, multiply that number by .65 (you can go as high as .75 if you are physically fit.) You want to get your heart rate to that level for at least 20 minutes three times per week.

Check out the web for ways to learn how to measure your heart rate. Or, a better solution is to ask your doctor about what your maximum heart rate target should be. When doing this level, it should be difficult to talk but not so bad that you feel exhausted.

Strength Training

While aerobic training is important, so is that of strength training. Don't worry; you don't have to work out so that you have bulging muscles. But, you do need to have some exercise regimen that incorporates building your muscle mass.

Strength training is actually the use of weights and movements that will increase the size and function of the muscles in your body. Although some individuals only think of strength training as weight training, the two are completely different. You don't want to over develop your muscle groups, but you do want to increase them in the way of health.

Increasing your muscle mass is important for a number of reasons. The key element will be to help you to maintain a healthy weight. You see, lean muscle mass, which is the type of muscle that you develop through strength training, is actually better at burning through stored fat. It also is helpful at burning calories faster. The combination means that they can help you to get rid of stored fat that you have throughout your body.

In technical terms, when you add additional muscle mass to your body, it is able to be more metabolically active than that of the fat that is stored in your body.

By increasing your muscle mass, you increase your metabolism as well. That means that your body remains lean and trim, which is ideal for heart health as well as overall organ health.

But, what if you don't have weight to lose? Even when you do drop to your ideal weight or if you are already there, it is still quite important for you to take care of these aspects for other health reasons.

Lean muscle mass is important for optimum health. Your body, especially your muscles, is trim and they can then pump blood easier. In addition, they are less likely to be injured or to develop problems later in life. The longer that your muscle groups are healthy, the longer that the rest of your body does well.

If you end up being in a sedentary lifestyle because of injuries and just lack of energy (something else that is a benefit from strength training) you can end up with countless health conditions that go along with it.

In addition to all of this, strength training also aids in keeping the heart strong. With the right training, you can increase the pumping power of the heart.

How much strength training you do depends on your needs for weight loss and your current muscle condition. One of the best things to do to gain both this type of exercise as well as aerobic is to join a gym or visit your local recreation center where you can work out weekly.

Again, with strength training like that of aerobic training, a regimen of three times per week is ideal for weight benefit and muscle training benefits.

Keeping each of these functions of your body healthy is something that you absolutely need to do. But, even with aerobic training as well as strength training, there is more that you'll need to tackle to complete the entire exercise package.

Flexibility Training

Believe it or not, you have to do your stretching. Stretching is yet another key function of improving your health and well-being. One of the key reasons that you need to use flexibility training is that of keeping your joints healthy.

Did you know that the onset of arthritis can start any time after the age of 25 (even younger sometimes)?

The arthritis that you feel now is only going to get worse and since it is a degenerative disease, it is likely to leave you with deformed, disabled joints. But, with the help of flexibility training now, you can avoid these conditions all together.

Flexibility training keeps you moving right. By stretching, you help your muscles to stretch and therefore keep them from getting hurt. Your muscles become lithe and limber. You can move like you did when you were in your 20's, accomplishing the things that you want and need to do. When you increase your body's ability to move in all directions, you feel younger and your body is actually improving in age, too.

Stretching and toning your muscles and joints is an important part of improving your overall health. With this type of training, you can keep your joints working optimally and you reduce your risk of strains, pulls and sprains significantly.

One of the most common complaints today from the Baby Boomer age is that of back pain. No matter what you may have done to it or what you think is wrong with it, back pain is a very common condition that happens more and more as you age.

But, when you add in a strength training workout to your exercise regimen, you improve the quality of those muscles and increase your spinal's movement and flexibility. You actually reduce the pain that you may be in and even prevent further injuries from happening to your back or hips, yet another common pain location for the Baby Boomers today.

A flexibility training regimen should be done at least 3 times per week for 20 minutes at a time. If you want to see rapid improvement here, you should try to do some form of stretching each morning and each evening. Just a few minutes of doing this will increase your body's tone and flexibility and it's a great way to start and end the day!

Pulling It All Together

Now, does all of that sound like it is just too much to do? It doesn't have to be.

In fact, really all you need is just 1 hour three times per week. Or, you can break apart these workouts to give yourself less of a lump of time commitment. You need:

- 20 minutes of aerobic training for heart health three times per week.

- 20 minutes of strength training for muscle improvement three times per week.

- 20 minutes of flexibility training for movement and joint improvement, three times per week.

A great way to gain these benefits is to invest in a membership to a gym. To help you to get started, work with a personal trainer, telling them what your goals are. You don't have to continue working with them but after a month or so of training, you'll be able to do your workout routine on your own. Just don't falter from it or you'll have to start all over again.

For flexibility training, consider taking in a yoga class or another type of easy movement training. This too is something that you can learn and then do on your own if you would like to.

When you do these things, you get to transform your life in so many ways. Consider the people that you know that are over the age of 60. When you meet John and he shakes your hand, do you feel how weak and frail it is? Do you feel his bones and realize that this once very large and tough man is now frail and very weak. You may even feel like you could break his hand if you hold onto it too hard.

Is that the type of handshake that you want to give? Or, do you want to be able to firmly grasp someone's hand and feel the strength coming through? When you incorporate an exercise regimen like this, you can gain those benefits and so much more.

In addition to this, exercise can actually help to improve your age. Aerobic training as well as strength training helps to stimulate your body to produce growth hormone. This hormone is a key ingredient to improving the health of your individual cells. If you remember, improving each of your cells is important in keeping yourself healthy longer.

Therefore, when your body produces more growth hormone, it can actually reverse the aging that your body has already gone through. That's because growth hormone actually can restore the health and the youth of each of your cells.

One important thing to realize from this is that through exercising, you can improve much if not all of the damage that you've done to your body over the years. You can restore your youth to a degree and then maintain it for some time to come.

Exercise simply must be a part of your life. The Baby Boomer requires this type of movement for benefits that come later on in life, too.

CHAPTER 9 - YOUR FINANCIAL WOES

One of the largest worries that a baby boomer has to deal with is the financial aspect of life. It may seem strange to include the money aspect of your life in this e-book, but the Baby Boomer needs to take into account the financial obstacles that they are beginning to experience.

Many baby boomers are already seeing the financial crunch as they watch their parents struggle to pay the bills. Some of them are seeing that their parent's homes are being reversed mortgaged to pay them something back so that they can actually afford daily life. Even worse, should they need long term health care and end of life care, they aren't sure of just how that's going to be paid for.

But, there is a problem. The Baby Boomer generation is also the generation that changed the world with their care free attitude. They started their lives in a post war period that was quite prosperous, didn't have to worry about saving because many of the years have been economically beneficial to them. And, now, most baby boomers don't have the funds that will allow them to retire.

The Baby Boomer's Guide to Life after Retirement

Baby boomers liked to spend, and they spent more than any other generation before them. They also liked to mortgage real estate, run up credit cards and even have started more businesses than any other generation.

What does all of this mean to you, though?

As a Baby Boomer, is it incredibly important for you to invest the time and money into looking at your financial situation.

The first thing you need to address is how long you'll be working. Many Baby Boomers plan to work longer. Since this generation has aged well to this point, they are expected to live longer. But, that doesn't mean that they will be leaving their jobs at the standard age of 65 which is what Social Security allows them to do.

Instead, many of them, more than half, will continue to work longer. Some will retire only to work part time, start their own business or work without pay. The smallest percentage of Baby Boomers plans to never work again after they retire.

The question is what can you financially do?

Many of your parents didn't spend their time determining just how expensive it will be to afford health care and even more so the cost of living that is today. For that reason, many more are living off of Social Security, help from family and even elderly care services.

But, you don't have to find yourself in this position. Here are some tips that can help you to get your finances in order so that you can work or not work at your leisure when you reach your retirement.

- Savings. The largest component of being able to live well after you retire is the money that you have in the bank. Of course, if you haven't started saving at this point, you still should be considering it. The payments that will come in from Social Security are likely to be quite low in comparison to the lifestyles that most Baby Boomers live today.

- Spending. Many Baby Boomers like to spend. But, now is the time to reel that in some so that you can afford to spend longer into your future.

- Determine what pension, 401k or other type of investment you have and manage it. It will be incredibly important for you to learn how these funds are doing. As you approach retirement, you'll need to readjust the funds to be more conservative so that you don't lose it all.

- Invest wisely. Although there is plenty of time to invest and see a nice return, it is also something that should mean more risk to you now. You'll want to do the research needed and work on your risk tolerance to determine the best opportunity for you.

The Key to Success

Since each financial outlook is different from one Baby Boomer to the next, one of the most beneficial tasks that you can take on is to find a financial advisor. While we have talked a lot about the things that you can do to improve your life's longevity, you need someone that can financially make that possible. A skilled financial advisor will provide you with the knowledge to make the right decisions, ultimately.

They can help you to determine how to spend, invest and save your funds. They can help to develop a strategy that will allow you to fund the lifestyle that you are living today well into the future.

Working with you, they will help you to find out what things you can do differently now, so that the financial reward comes later.

What You Need To Plan For

What you may not realize is just what you need to plan for. With the longevity that you'll get from being healthy, you will need funds that will take you through your entire life. If you have a lifestyle that you are comfortable with right now, you'll want to maintain that in the coming years as well. With financial advice, that can happen.

In addition to this, more and more people are looking at traveling, exploring the world and enjoying the luxuries that life has to offer. With this also comes an added cost. While these things are excellent tools to keep your mind stimulated and your body healthy, you'll need to be able to afford them.

In addition, there is health care to consider. With the rising costs of just stepping foot into a doctor's office, it is becoming increasingly important to find a way to afford this too. The risk of counting on insurance companies or government funded medical care is quite limiting and can often place you where you don't want to be.

Even still, many Baby Boomers still have homes to pay off that are mortgaged at least one time. This means that you'll need to be able to make enough to use this money wisely. While there are options like reverse mortgages that allow you to be paid a sum of your home's value each month, this comes at a high price and may not be the right decision for your needs.

Beyond anything else, the Baby Boomer generation is one that likes to live life on his own pace and likes to do things their own way.

Julius Greene

Having changed the world, you may just need some extra funds to make that continue, too.

If you are a Baby Boomer, it is time now to make the decisions regarding your finances for the future. If you don't make these critical decisions now, then the funds won't be there when you need them.

Invest your time and money into a solid, trusted financial advisor that you can work one on one with. Learn what they can offer to you and find out just what it is that you can expect from them. With the dedication of these individuals, you will quickly find your place in the financial lifestyle you want to live.

The Baby Boomer must address money concerns now, while they are healthy and while they have the time to make changes. To live a prosperous life, you need to manage the financial aspect of it as well as the health aspects.

Yet, this doesn't have to be difficult with the right people by your side to make it happen.

Chapter 10 - A Lifestyle Makeover is Key to a Longer Life

One of the most difficult things for the Baby Boomer to change is that of his lifestyle. That's why we've left it until now. You knew it was coming. You have to give up drinking, smoking and all of those other things that are ripping apart your health and well-being. We don't have to tell you those things, but if you don't do them, nothing you've learned here is going to prolong your life any more than they will shorten it.

But, lifestyle changes don't have to be for the bad. There are actually many small things that you can do to improve the overall quality and health of your life without having to give up the things you love.

On the other hand, there are those things that you do have to take into consideration and repair. You do have to set your priorities straight and you do have to make sure that your health becomes the most important thing in the world to you. That's no short order.

And, we'll start with the hardest yet most important one of all.

Stress

Baby Boomers are known for the stress that they are under on a constant basis. Challenge is something that many of you live for. In fact, more than 40 percent of the Baby Boomer generation will continue to work not for the money but for the mental stimulation and challenge that it provides to them.

Nevertheless, stress can be detrimental to your overall well-being. In fact, it will shorten your life span if you don't do something about it right now.

Why does stress play such an important role in your life? There are a number of reasons why, but when it comes to what stress does to your body physically, the evidence is in.

Stress is known as the silent killer because it affects virtually every part of your body. Not only does it cause trauma to your brain, but it will cause muscles and joints to become injured, organs to not work as well and allows your body to remain open to illness.

In addition, it helps you to age faster. Because stress increases the amount of cortisol that your body produces, you age faster. Cortisol is an element that actually increases the speed at which you age. The longer and more severe the stress is, the more damage it does to you.

The good news is that most of the damage that comes from stress can be repaired and even elevated. But, this does mean that you need to make some lifestyle changes now to make that happen for you.

For starters, stressful situations like work environments that are negative or cause you to remain in a state of stress are not good for you and should be changed. Although you may not believe that you can do this, the stress you face there will shorten your lifespan and worsen your health in the short and long term.

Here are some ways that you can reduce stress even when you can't leave the job behind.

- Physical activity will help to reduce stress. Going for a walk, playing a sport, and even the exercise that you get in your Baby Boomer exercise regimen will all help. By pumping oxygen rich blood throughout your stressed muscles, you improve the overall function of them and therefore help your body to relax.

- Mental relaxation can also help. Learn how to do yoga (remember it's great for stretching too!) or you can learn to meditate. You can also find other quiet activities that can help to relax you.

- Take on a new learning experience. Learn how to do karate, meet new people and expand your knowledge base through reading. Finding these things to do will encourage your brain to work more successfully and it will encourage stress relief.

- Do things that you enjoy. Getting a massage will help to melt away stress. Go for a walk or go swimming. Spend time with family and friends just playing a game. These small things make a considerable difference in stress reduction.

Julius Greene

But, stress isn't all that you need to take into consideration when it comes to lifestyle changes.

Beat the Bad Habits

As mentioned, those habits that are bad for you, such as smoking, drinking alcohol and illegal substances should not be done. The sooner that you stop doing so, the better it can be. The good news is that some of the damage from smoking will repair itself on its own. But, alcohol damage won't be so lucky.

Even if you need a cigarette to relax, the bottom line is that smoking and drinking will lead to cancers of the lungs, brain cell deterioration and much more. The circulatory system alone suffers greatly at these risks.

There are many helpful groups available today, that your doctor can help you to find that can help you to make these changes so that they aren't too hard to do or too taxing on your daily life.

Positive Attitude

Be happy. In short, improving your mood and giving yourself more opportunities to be positive can also help to increase your longevity and help you to remain healthy, longer. Although doctors don't fully understand why, many patients that that face life threatening conditions that have a positive attitude going in are the ones that actually pull through. Even in the worst of situations, having this full of life, positive mental attitude can pull you through when even medicine can fail.

To stay positive, you should do things that you enjoy. Since most Baby Boomers are still working, that means cutting back those hours a bit and enjoying a picnic in the park, relaxing after dinner and just enjoying the peace of the afternoon. Catch a nap, call and talk to a friend for an hour about nothing and even spend the day laughing and carrying on.

Doing things that you enjoy doing is beneficial to your overall health. As we mentioned earlier, it helps to stimulate the brain. But, it also helps to improve your quality of life. Let's face it, nothing that you learned here can be beneficial to you if your quality of life is minimized in any way.

Getting through the difficult times is hard to do and still stay positive. Some find the hope and help they need in religion, while others seek out answers in science. Even still, many just look at the benefits and blessings they have now and hope they continue for a long time in coming.

Doing whatever it takes to improve your lifestyle will ultimately lead you to a lifestyle that is positive and overall beneficial to your goal of a long, prosperous lifestyle.

Personalize this To-Do List

Now that you have the necessary information, get moving on implementing each one of the changes that we've covered here. Here's a checklist to help you to find those rewards now.

- Improve your diet today. Develop an eating plan that helps to promote longevity and health. Detach from eating for emotional support. Reaffirm your connection with a long life instead.

- Start to move. The exercise regimen that includes strength training, aerobic exercise and flexibility training will improve virtually any health condition you may be in.

Julius Greene

- Improve your brain power. Include stimulating activities into your life daily to encourage your brain to keep growing and expanding instead of shutting down.

- Take the time to consider supplementation and hormone changes that can ultimately encourage your body to live longer, healthier as well as to look amazing while you do it.

- Get your finances in order.

- Improve your lifestyle by cutting out the bad including the silent killer that stress is.

Chapter 11 - Where Will Retirement Find You?

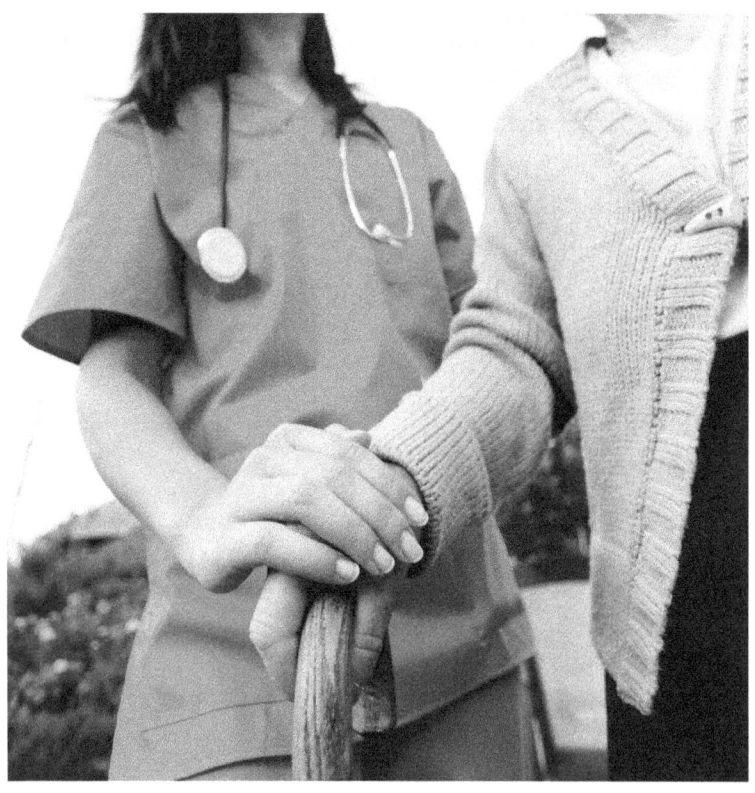

Close to 78 million baby boomers were said to have contributed to the population crisis of sorts experienced in America between 1946 and 1964. Apart from the growing economic stability and increased financial prosperity enjoyed by the survivors, families to which baby boomers were born into were keen to give them the best of everything as they felt blessed to have the children and having survived the aftermath of war; thus, the baby boomer generation acquired privileges of better education, higher number of college degrees, more freedom to explore, learn and cultivate new political ideologies, question authority and be aware of their cultural and civil rights. This was the generation that fought up for the under-privileged lot of students who were discriminated against in colleges and professional institutions; the baby boomers shaped much of the America we see today and African-American people can thank them for paving a path for their progress in the US today.

Music – it was a changing as was the cultural norms that were frequently questioned by the baby boomers during their teenage and college years; even as young adults, they showed a keen affinity to copying the dressing style of their favorite rock-stars and musicians and blues jeans and tees became a uniform code for them, which still stands today. This soon gave way to Rhythm and Blues once Rock and Roll had firmly been established.

But, the large percentage of retirement-age baby boomers today (close to 29% of the American population) are more aware than the previous generation about saving and still enjoying for and after retirement, so are focusing more on taking care of health benefits, privately (through insurance) and aiming to raise the issue of government aided Medical and Social Security for them.

Once the sole contributors of the US government's high and sustained financial income, baby boomers who were high achievers in their chosen professions as well as business and military heads were responsible for empowering the United States with the kind of financial stability it required to also offer aid to European and other world communities; however, once they retire, there are bound to be lesser people in the US workforce and higher number of professional retirees. This may signify the US government having to finance the retirement options of baby boomers in part so they can accommodate the remaining generation of retirees later on, with better and more advanced healthcare and facilities.

Various plots of land for retirement homes, colonies and societies have been marked off the US government as well as some private agencies who are making these available for the baby boomers reaching retirement-age; these retirees are equipped with added Social Security and Medicare programs so are better able to afford the best of town-houses with frills of cultural and social zones, much like resorts and retirement becomes a time of relaxation and rejuvenation for the baby boomers, then.

Reunite with Other Baby Boomers in Retirement Communities

Having the advantage of prosperous parents meeting all their needs for higher education, better lifestyles and more freedom during developmental years meant baby boomers were equipped to face life on their own terms: flouting conventions, questioning established rules, bringing in new political thoughts and working towards radical change in the corporate community. This lead to a sense of higher goal settings and ability to reach them too, since baby boomers were a privileged lot.

Subsequently, their desires were always more than that of their parents: so independent, dominant and powerful positions enjoyed by the baby boomer generation at work and the success that can with it naturally guided them towards finding ways to maintain use of their creative energies usefully, even post-retirement, which brings us to the topic of raising quality of life for baby boomers via community action and other such programs.

Trying to find ways to ensure an active lifestyle even after retirement became important for those professionals belonging to the baby boomers generation more because they followed a creed of shunning the aging process and finding ways to stay young, through a deliberate disciplining of their body – then be it exercise and fitness routines that nearly broke their hips or using advanced collagen treatments to reverse the aging process, this generation tried it all!

Julius Greene

Baby boomers developed confidence, the need to question authority and the establishment, got all their needs met by affluent parents and thus emerged an aware, highly qualified and hip lot of adults that easily got accustomed to communities around them recognizing their worth as much as they themselves did. Bill Parks, a former architecture director of Del Webb Corporation, predicts that the future sees many developers retiring and leading active post-retirement lives to benefit the adult community, of which there are over 1,200 country-wide – and others on the anvil.

The advantages of these post-retirement adult communities for baby boomers includes giving them a place to rest, relax and rejuvenate and then empowering them some to fend off the after-effects of an empty nest syndrome by giving them luxurious lifestyles and quality healthcare even after their current lifestyles have always managed to combine location, atmosphere, enviable sizing and best facilities always.

There are senior housing councils in the US that reveal mind-boggling figures like 207, 000 retired and qualified baby boomers availing the establishments in over 55 communities for about 1/5th of the 1.1 million purchases of new homes in 2003! Nearly $51 billion in sales were generated by these new homes owned by the baby boomers, so their planning was definitely in place!

Places like Arizona, Florida and sunny California were favored by the baby boomers looking for adult communities that provided for active lifestyles post-retirement –and they could well afford the lush golf courses, pools and country club memberships with the work they'd all put in that generated surplus wealth for their golden years.

These retirement communities for the baby boomers and those enjoyed by their parents differ greatly in the facilities offered and expected: the earlier lot were not too keen on the existence of fitness villages but the baby boomers were obsessive about working out and staying fit (read reversing aging effectively), so didn't mind paying elite estate developers a fortune for near-resort like amenities and staying in close proximity of urban centers, such as the Sunbelt.

The current situation for retirement-age baby boomers is that the prohibitive price tag of living along the Sunbelt ($150,000 at the start for a 2BHK town home) has taken them further from the sunny climes in exchange for better health care as opposed to simply means of entertainment offered by the retirement adult communities enjoyed by the older generation.

Spend Your Days in Different Parts of the Globe

For regular people, cost of travel and the time it calls for to be taken away from work can be two main hindrances to considering travel for themselves, what with competition and inflation setting in as well for them; however, with baby boomers – born into privileged, wealthy families that showered them with everything they needed and the greater freedom they enjoyed in exercising choices, there's no such obstacles.

This is because baby boomers are products of the population explosion after the Second World War (the period between 1946 and 1958, to be precise) when America and other parts of Europe witnessed a surge in childbirth rates, following the economic prosperity and stability enjoyed by the surviving families who could pass these on to their children.

Thus, baby boomers are actually the target audience of many exclusive and up-market tour operators who wait and plan their packages and schemes around the interests and needs of the baby boomers approaching retirement, who can jolly well afford to do so as they have already come from wealthy families; added to that they have held high income jobs, been high achievers and do not need to worry about these or looking after families that are well taken care of, so are free to travel.

They also have an independent streak in them that does not permit them to take the ways of the older generation when they faced retirement i.e. sulking at home or worrying over approaching old age since they have already considered how to fight aging (through exercise and fitness routines besides taking advantage of medical science treatments for collagen, knee and hip replacements etc.) so can concentrate on availing the benefits of a great travel deal they can easily afford.

The attention they enjoyed as kids has continued for the baby boomers through their adulthood and even till their retirement age as recently travel companies hoping to entice them with luxury travel options have further travel agencies luring this deep-pocketed lot with an exclusive website catering only to baby boomer travel needs, interests, amenities and customized travel plans requested. Just an email dropped in for enquiry will start the process of online booking of travel deals, checking and comparing options on other sites and many will do this till late at night since they are comfortable handling technology and gadgets that allow them to view, review, compare, scan and print essential documents —even tickets and guides off the Internet.

Thus, the true nature of baby boomers at retirement age is to opt for a relaxing and illuminating vacation at luxury resorts or hotels rather than the general touristy choice of a wayside hotel that is overcrowded; they feel they can splurge their hard earned dollars and they deserve to do so on themselves and a certain degree of comfort and frills. With the US home to 29% baby boomers, the travel industry there can look forward to hundreds of booking provided they learn about specific interests, comfort levels, can pamper customers that are accustomed to being treated well and give them variety, fun and luxury travel plans.

Chapter 12 - Baby Boomer Grandparents

Parents are very important in the life of a child, yet grandparents are more special than parents can ever be. The most cherished memories of an adult are of those times spent in the charming companies of grandparents.

Baby boomers seem to be ever youthful. They also have a great passion for living. They seem to have arrived on earth with a vision and a mission of creating a different type of society. Baby boomers have exhibited immense initiative in all aspects of life, and their activities have had a great impact on American society, so much so that the America of today does not even remotely resemble the America of the fifties or sixties.

Life has challenged baby boomers in a number of ways. Baby boomer parents created a different type of bond with their children. They participated in the lives of their kids more than any generation of the past. Baby boomer parents tried to be not only a parent, but also best friends to their children. Though the results of this are not completely positive, children did value family life and emulate the qualities of their parents much more than the younger generations of the past did. For baby boomers, parenting was a great mission.

When baby boomers became grandparents, they understood the meaning of having grandchildren. This generation, which had resisted the onset of adulthood itself, must have found it difficult indeed to accept the realities of aging. However, they quickly accepted the roles of wise and kind grandparents. They played a great role not only in the lives of their grandchildren, but also in the lives of their children by offering their insight and guidance on various matters related to life.

Children view grandparents differently. They love grandparents and enjoy any opportunity to visit them even if it is for the simple reason that grandmother had baked a fresh batch of cookies. Sitting on grandfather's lap and listening to his stories or simply enjoying his company is a part of childhood that all children enjoy and cherish in their memories when they grow up. Even baby boomer grandparents enjoy these moments of intimacy with their grandchildren.

In many ways, being a grandparent is a much more fulfilling experience than being a parent. Children enjoy listening to the wise words of their grandparents. Life with grandparents also makes them feel secure, something that life with parents doesn't. On the laps of grandparents, grandchildren learn that it is possible to achieve success in life and that the fun does not cease even when you are old and a grandparent. Children intuitively know that there a number of life values and lessons to be learnt on the laps of grandparents. Throughout their lives, they nurture the lessons thus learned from an elderly person.

Baby boomers enjoy this new role just as they enjoyed their role as parents. They accepted the challenge of parenthood with a passion that almost redefined the concept of parenting. They have brought that same passion to their role as grandparents. Baby boomers can transmit their passion for life, their love and commitment for family life to their children and grandchildren. Thus they become the greatest gift a child can ever have, a wise grandpa and grandma who not only love them, but are also great fun to be with.

As baby boomer grandparents, the time you spend with your grandchildren is a wonderful time to pass on the wisdom of half a century to the younger generation. Children need their parent's guidance and knowledge; simultaneously, parents also tend to be teachers and strict disciplinarians. Relationship with grandparents is much easier and stress free and children can really open themselves to their grandparents. No wonder they view grandparents as sources of love and wisdom.

The Baby Boomer Grandparent's Role in the Toy Market

Surveys reveal the fact that more and more baby boomers are becoming grandparents and purchasing toys as gifts for their grandchildren. Baby boomer grandparents, therefore, are responsible for the large profits that the toy manufacturers make.

Aging baby boomers, which once spend a delightful childhood playing with their favorite toys, are now spending a lot on toys for their grandchildren. This tendency on the part of the baby boomers has helped toy manufacturers make colossal profits.

As per the predictions made by certain consultants, the following four years will see about 10 million grandparents. The number of grandparents increases every year. The largest number of grandparents is those who were born in 1957, a year noted by demographers for its largest number of births.

As per a survey, people above the age of 50 control around 70 percent of the wealth of America. Surveys have also shown that grandparents spend around 500 dollars per year on a single grandchild. The total amount of money that grandparents spend on their grandchildren is 30 million dollars every year. About 25 percent of the toys are, therefore, purchased by grandparents.

Activities of Companies to Attract Baby Boomer Grandparents

According to Kevin Curran, the general manager and senior vice-president of Fisher-Price, the rise in the sale of it toys can be attributed only to the rising number of grandparents. This company manufactures and sells toys that are more old-fashioned than those manufactured by other companies. Toys such as "Little People," about forty-five years old, have broken sales records. Fisher-Price also publishes a magazine called "Loving Your Grandbaby," in a bid to attract aged buyers.

KB Toys has launched the Grandparents' Rewards Club, which aims at selling toys to grandparents at a 10 percent discount every Tuesday. This sales event is conducted in three venues in Houston-- Baybrook, Almeda, and Willowbrook malls. KB toys developed this sales strategy because it was very much aware that a large segment of its consumers comprised baby boomer grandparents.

Sababa Toys aims at bringing back classic toys to the market in order to attract baby boomer grandparents. Sababa products include Grandparent's Treasure Chest Scrapbook, wood puzzles, and toys that promote learning such as Big Brain Academy and Brain Age.

Julius Greene
How Do Boomer Grandparents Select Toys?

Baby boomer grandparents prefer toys of a certain category. They are interested in toys that promote learning and creativity, especially in art and music, toys that evoke memories of the past such as Price's Telephone and Snoopy Sniffer, and also contemporary toys such as Kid-Tough Digital Camera, a technology-driven toy that enables grandchildren to send digital photographs via e-mail to their grandparents while they are on holiday. Baby boomer grandparents are more comfortable with modern technology than any other generation. They are at ease when they purchase modern, technology-driven gadgets.

Some baby boomer grandparents take special care in selecting the toys they want their grandchildren to have. They rightly realize that children appreciate gifts such as Internet games, iPods, and CDs. However, baby boomer grandparents are not that particular about purchasing these items because they know that the kids will get it anyhow. Baby boomer grandparents are more particular about their grandchildren experiencing the same type of childhood they once enjoyed--exploring the environment, playing social games, and riding bikes with family members.

Unique Nature of Baby Boomer Grandparents

While parents give children toys in order to promote learning and creativity, baby boomer grandparents wish to promote learning in their grandchildren in unique ways. They want to instill in their grandchild a love of nature and an awareness of global issues. They want to give quality time to their grandchildren so that the kids would learn about the value of family. During the kids birthdays or at Christmas, they prefer to purchase toys such as science project kits.

The Baby Boomer's Guide to Life after Retirement

The generation of baby boomers has a unique history. Since the parents of baby boomers had just survived the Second World War, they wanted to ensure a safe and happy life for their children. Now, the grandchildren and children of these baby boomers have the best that life can offer them. Baby boomer grandparents wish to gift toys to their grandchildren as a means of going back to their own childhood days.

The character of baby boomers is just as unique as their history. They desire their grandchildren to focus on achievements and education. Baby boomers went to college and got a college degree with a strong belief that anything is possible in life. They have taught the same attitude toward life to their grandchildren too.

The toy industry is now targeting baby boomer grandparents more and more. Their love for their grandchildren, their affluence, and the fact that they have spent their money more powerfully than any other generation in the history of America are reasons for this.

CHAPTER 13 - THE 6 BABY BOOMER COMMANDMENTS

The baby boomers are a unique generation and have created a different culture. There are six rules that most baby boomers are defined by.

The baby boom generation marks a group of nearly 20 years where the birth rate rose dramatically and over 77 million babies were born. Since then, the birth rate has returned to normal, but the influx of people into society was astronomical. The baby boom generation has been an important part of the American culture. They have defined many of the current beliefs, became law makers and politicians and have served this country.

The Baby Boomer's Guide to Life after Retirement

However those born between 1946 and 1967 haven't always been given the best monikers. They have been considered self-righteous and self-indulgent being the complete opposites of their parents who sacrificed to make their way in the world.

Baby boomers have fought against the negative stereotypes. Baby boomers lived through a time that was vastly different than any other. They saw pointless wars being fought, destroying lives and family. They fought to relieve their families of poverty while trying to gain education to create a better lifestyle.

The ideals of this generation created The Boomer's Six Commandment. These "rules" defined what the baby boomer generation was about and how they lived. Most of those born during this era followed these ideals, but not all. Every generation is defined by the circumstances and experiences they have to deal with. Think about everything that happened in those years: Vietnam War, Civil Right Movement and the Energy Crisis.

1. Be trendy and hip. Some think a major problem with the baby boomers is not being able to grow up. This is seen in a variety of ways. There are those who try to reverse the aging problem, which will never put plastic surgeons out of business. Baby boomers sometimes get frozen in their own era, dressing and acting like they have for 20 years. However, there are other baby boomers that move on with the fashion times, wearing and exemplifying what it means to be cool.

2. Being relevant is important, so accept the changes. Everything moves on and even the baby boomers couldn't keep the culture stagnant. They learned wisely that it is more important to accept the culture that is changing around them rather than fight it. This can be seen through many different ideals of the baby boomers.

3. Be an individual. There were so many children born in that time period that it is easy to lump everyone into one category. However, the baby boomers won't allow that. Being an individual is just as important as supporting the greater good. The baby boomers lived through a time of enormous change and have created radical movements that have transformed this country.

4. Create a new history. What happened in the past doesn't seem to matter to baby boomers. Everything they did was done for the first time, at least that is what they all want you to believe. Baby boomers view their generation as a milestone creator leaving no room for any previous generation to have a significant importance. Occasions that happened in the past are just that – history – and have no place their lives.

5. Don't be a sellout. If you become a sellout, you will lose your baby boomer card. Just because they are living the American dream as white, middle-class folks don't mean that is what they feel deep down in their heart. They will always be revolutionaries who are willing to change a generation at the drop of a hat.

6. Always question authority. Baby boomers had a difficult time of trusting anyone older than them. It meant they wouldn't listen to cops, priests or their parents. This was the care-free generation who couldn't trust anyone, just each other. Baby boomers didn't follow the rules, they made the rules. They weren't going to be told how to live their lives.

About The Author

Julius Greene is a grandson of a baby boomer. He grew up with his grandfather when his parents died in a tragic car accident.

Julius is a graduate of BA Journalism and is a fulltime journalist. His stories are usually seen at the front page of the local newspaper in Detroit.

www.ingramcontent.com/pod-product-compliance
Lightning Source LLC
Chambersburg PA
CBHW070811220526
45466CB00002B/639